TODAY

I AM...

Jo,
May the Joy of
Today...
keep you in peace,
good health &
much happiness
Your friend
Patricia Latcher
9/24/2019

ALSO FROM PATRICIA L. ATCHISON

CHILDREN'S BOOKS
Little Blue Penguin; McKenzie's Frosty Surprise

HOW TO GUIDES
How to Write For Children,
An Easy Three Step Guide to Writing Children's Books

CONTRIBUTING AUTHOR WORKS
The Book Of Emotions Or - how it feels to feel.

FOLLOW PATRICIA L. ATCHISON

WEBSITE
www.patriciaatchisonauthor.com

FACEBOOK
@PatriciaLAtchison
www.facebook.com/PatriciaLAtchison

TWITTER
@atchison_author
www.twitter.com/atchison_author

PINTEREST
www.pinterest.ca/platchison

INSTAGRAM
www.instagram.com/patricial.atchison

LINKEDIN
www.linkedin.com/in/patricialatchison

TODAY I AM...

AN EMPOWERING JOURNAL BACK TO SELF

FEATURING CREATIVE PRACTICES TO ENGAGE THE MIND AND SPIRIT

CELEBRATING YOU TODAY

Patricia L. Atchison

Wood Lily Publishers
Airdrie, Alberta, Canada

TODAY I AM...

AN EMPOWERING JOURNAL BACK TO SELF

By Patricia L. Atchison

Copyright © 2019 Patricia L. Atchison

First Printing: 2019

Wood Lily Publishers
Airdrie, Alberta, Canada
Copyright © 2019 Patricia L. Atchison

ISBN: 978-0-9783369-5-0

The information, practices, exercises, ideas, and strategies contained herein may not be suitable for all situations. The author does not claim to have validated or verified any information within. Be sure to consult a professional where required.

TODAY I AM...

AN EAGLE SOARING
ACROSS THE SKIES,
ONE WITH THE PATTERNS
OF THE EARTH;
MY EYES SEARCHING,
MY HEART BEATING,
WITH ANTICIPATION
OF WHAT I MIGHT FIND.

To all who have soared before me
in search of knowledge and answers,
thank you for your light, love and sharing.

Patricia L. Atchison

Content

Author Musings

About This Empowering Journal Back to Self

Five years ago, after struggling through a time of depression, I asked myself, "Who am I?". I realized I had lost me! That person I once knew as a young adult, in midlife years and beyond had disappeared. I didn't know who I was anymore. In continually doing for my husband, doing for my child, doing for my parents, doing for my community, I wasn't doing for myself and could never say 'no' to anyone. I rarely gave myself permission for 'me' time and the energy to do for me, and when I did, I felt guilty and stressed about it.

Through the years, I had lost the essence of myself, and with it came feelings of regret, self-criticism, depression, loss of self-esteem, and confidence. I knew I had to find a way back to whom I once was, a better version, or at the very least get to know 'me' again.

The practices listed in this journal are ones that either came to me from The Universe (I often receive inspiration at 4:00 am) and some I learned as I went along, by attending self-help, growth, and spiritual sessions. The biggest change for me was learning gratitude, being grateful, and applying it in everyday life. My outlook and focus improved over time.

I started writing the quotes you see throughout this journal when they came to me as inspiration in the early hours of the morning. I knew I wanted to share them, but until recently didn't know how. The idea for this journal also came to me the same way.

In sharing these practices, it is my goal to help you become aware of the world surrounding 'you' at the moment and how to view each 'Today' with new promise, gratitude, positivity, light, and love. Create space in your life to fill your heart with love, and get to know you again.

IF YOU FEEL YOU'VE LOST SIGHT OF WHO YOU ARE (OR ONCE WERE), THEN THIS JOURNAL IS FOR YOU!

About The Author Quotes

I'm the type of writer who has little notebooks in drawers around the house, specifically in the bathroom vanity. I find during the night, and early morning, when inspiration comes to me, I need to write down my ideas quickly before I forget them. When I started my journey out of despair and into the light, I would awake in the morning with a "Today I am...", inspirational phrase in mind. I started jotting each one down. Some days insights didn't arrive, and now they merely come on occasion. The quotes you'll find in this journal were created those early morning hours over a year or two.

TODAY...

THE FUTURE SEEMS DARK AND FOREBODING

LIKE AN UNKNOWN FOREST PATH, BUT DEEP WITHIN

I SEE BEAMS OF BRIGHT SUNLIGHT PIERCING

THE SHADE AND LIGHTING THE WAY.

The Ideas Presented

I love research, learning, and using new tools. These are things I read on the Internet, newsletters I subscribe to, classes I've taken, women's circles attended, books read, etc. Some of the ideas presented here I learned from other sources, presenters, and teachers. It's sort of like when in passing, someone says something, and it makes a profound effect. Then, as you recall it in the future, you know why you needed to hear it or learn it, but you can't remember where the idea came from in the first place.

The following sections are brief summaries, which will lead you to the related practices as outlined later in this journal.

'Good to Know' ~ Definitions

Healing

Healing can come in many forms: Physician's diagnosis, surgery, and/or medications, Acupuncture, Chiropractic, Physiotherapy, Holistic and Natural practices, through nutrition and movement. The list is endless.

Healing can also come from within, by choices we make and whatever follow-up tools we require to help us be in the best mental and physical shape possible. Wellness is a mindset. Through a positive mindset, anything is possible. This journal provides the tools to help you, if you are willing, to find the positive, joyful, gratifying aspects of your life.

Grounding

Grounding is a term that runs throughout many healing circles. Physical grounding or 'Earthing' is taking your shoes and socks off outdoors and walking barefoot on grass. The body receives many health benefits from connecting to the earth energetically (look it up to learn more). My favorite place is a sandy beach or lush grassy park.

I've come up with a definition of grounding, which works for me. It means getting out of my head, and my surroundings and noise and settling into breath, being more authentically in my body in the present moment. It's like centering self, ignoring outside interference, receiving energy from within and becoming aware of my gifts and talents. It is from grounding that I can see me as I am, my visions, passions, and goals.

I talk about grounding here, because to do the exercises in this journal, to tune into yourself, it is important to ground yourself, eliminating outside world noise. Like a radio station sounding like static, grounding is tuning into self, eliminating the static, allowing you to hear 'You' clearer. Grounding needn't be experienced only outside. It can be done anywhere, anytime by simply sitting quietly and being conscious of going inside of 'self.'

TODAY...

CHANGE IS IMMINENT,
DON'T GET TOO COMFORTABLE.

Mindfulness

Mindfulness is a therapeutic practice used in spiritual circles. Mindfulness reminds us to return to the present moment and become aware of our feelings, thoughts, and body sensations, accepting what is without judgment or criticism. Outside of ourselves, we can also become mindful of the little things around us, such as the beauty of a sunrise, ice crystals in the air, a butterfly flitting about, or a colorful rainbow.

Being mindful is becoming conscious and aware. Take your breathing, for example. To become mindful is to recognize each breath as it enters your nose, fills your lungs, and exits the body completely. There is no thought as to how you are breathing, if it a good breath, did it supply the oxygen you needed, etc. It is merely a breath.

If you drive, have you ever had the experience of driving from one location to another and not really remember getting there? It's scary when you realize you were so wrapped up in a thought that you weren't conscious of how many stop signs or light intersections you went through. But somehow you arrived at your destination. Driving should be a mindful task where you are aware of every moment that you are in control of the wheel.

Life presents many 'little things' to us as gifts. Sometimes we are so consumed in living from one moment to the next without being mindful. If we are in this state, we miss all the little things that wake the senses and bring joy and fulfillment to our lives.

13

Intentions

I define an intention as an attitude or purpose of how I wish to align my life in the present moment. Setting an intention is powerful because it is what we hope to manifest, what we intend to attract or call into our life. Think of it as an aim, or something to commit to, that should come from the heart and be positive. Not everyone intends to be negative, so positivity is vital when setting your intention.

Intentions shift our mindset toward something we wish to manifest or call into our lives. Whether the aim comes true or not, we've set ourselves up to align our hearts and minds toward a definite purpose.

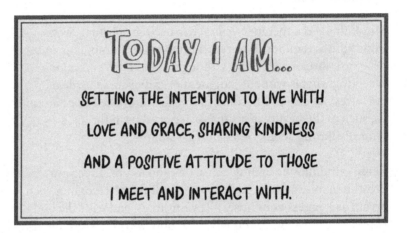

TODAY I AM...

SETTING THE INTENTION TO LIVE WITH

LOVE AND GRACE, SHARING KINDNESS

AND A POSITIVE ATTITUDE TO THOSE

I MEET AND INTERACT WITH.

Releasing

Any part of healing in one's life comes from the notion of releasing. Letting go of what no longer serves you. It's like holding on for 'dear life' to a life raft as it bounces along with a raging current. At some point, you can choose to jump off and swim to safety when the perfect opportunity presents itself, or you can decide to stay rooted to where you are, never budging, hoping that eventually you'll be saved somehow or other.

I personally choose to release and let go when I know I can no longer find joy where I'm at. The tools and practices presented in this journal will help you determine when it's time to release old thought patterns and move on to safety.

Positivity

It's not a hard lesson to learn that the more positive traits we have as human beings, the better things turn out to be in any given situation. Although not always the case, I would say it is mostly the case.

If you've been living in the negative (as I was) for many years, suddenly becoming uplifted is not reality. I discovered the tools in this journal have made all the difference to me in going from a negative, all is doom and gloom person, to a 'positive outlook' type of person.

If you are willing to change your perception from negative to positive possibilities as you read and practice some of the exercises in this journal, you'll find a shift to peace, joyfulness, and happiness.

Living in the Present

Do you know if you're living in the past, present, or future? I discovered the key to life is living in the present. I explain this concept in much more depth later on. For now, let it settle in your mind.

Living in the present is an excellent place to find peace, joy, and happiness, though not every moment in life will present itself as attractive, but we can learn to find special moments in the present as they come along.

Love for Self

The most improved choice you can make, which will have the best impact within your life is learning to love yourself!

This is not always easy, but using the exercises in this journal will aid you in accepting and loving yourself simply as you are. Keep this in mind as you journey through the learning practices throughout these pages.

TODAY'S
DREAMS ARE TOMORROW'S EXPERIENCES AND YESTERDAY'S MEMORIES!

The Power & Meaning of 'I AM'

Here is an exercise to bring focus to the power of 'you.' Find a quiet spot and do the following.

REPEAT OUT LOUD: **I AM**

LET THAT ROLL AROUND IN YOUR MIND FOR A MINUTE OR TWO.

REPEAT AGAIN WITH CONFIDENCE: I AM

TAKE A MOMENT TO LISTEN TO THE ECHO OF THOSE WORDS IN YOUR MIND.

REPEAT AGAIN WITH POWER: I AM

CAN YOU FEEL THE MAGNITUDE OF THOSE TWO WORDS?

When we add positive words to follow, I AM…, then we have a proclamation. A declaration to ourselves (first and foremost), then to anyone else who hears.

In this journal, I'm taking it one step further, and adding, TODAY I AM…, because as I explain in the next section, today is what we have, currently, right now, this is it, today!

TODAY I AM…, followed by positive thoughts (words and phrases) allows for an uplifted mindset.

Throughout these pages, you'll discover the power and pleasures of TODAY I AM….

WHERE IS YOUR MINDSET TODAY?

TODAY I AM...

DID YOU WRITE SOMETHING NEGATIVE?

WERE YOU HARD ON YOURSELF?

As an example: **TODAY I AM NOT HAPPY.**

When talking in 'TODAY I AM...' speak, you should select and write positive word choices to allow for healthy changes in your life. Like changing colors on a canvas, the brighter the words, the more vibrant the picture.

As an example: **TODAY I AM HAPPY.**

Okay, maybe you aren't happy at this immediate moment. However, by thinking, writing, and affirming that you are happy, a message is sent to your inner spirit and higher self. A suggestion that perhaps you can become satisfied in the next moment.

When I started my journey toward contentment, joy, and yes - happiness, it didn't happen overnight. It was a process of writing positive TODAY I AM... affirmations all the time.

In sharing these tools, with the intent that you will progress through them on your journey, I AM CONFIDENT you will discover the fantastic benefits of TODAY I AM....

TODAY I AM...

WORD-SMITHING MY WAY TO GREATNESS,

TO HEALING, TO JOY, TO FOCUS,

TO HEALTH AND HAPPINESS.

The Power of Three ~ Yesterday

TODAY...

I REMEMBER MY PAST WITH THE PURE PLEASURE OF VISITING AN OLD, BELOVED FRIEND.

Yesterday

If you do an Internet search in your browser on a poem called, "Yesterday Today and Tomorrow," you'll discover a sweet expression of these three simple words. My journey to joy became a discovery of learning what these words meant in my life.

I lived for the past, not necessarily because it was good, but because I was stuck there. I delved on memories I wished I could have changed. I relived happy moments, experiences, and people who once were in my life and wanted to have them back. The Universe has a way of teaching us what we need to become aware of, and I fatefully learned that if you live in the past all the time, you will be in a depressed state of mind.

I was living in the past and deeply depressed. My life's progression and the experiences I had been through were gone and no longer in my control. Any amount of thought about them wouldn't change anything, except dredging up old emotions. By using the practices I've presented in these pages, I managed to climb my way out of the dark hole I found myself in and guess what? I started to live in the future. I thought it was a better place to be.

NOTE: Use the grey areas throughout this journal to write your answers to the questions listed.

WHAT ARE YOUR THOUGHTS REGARDING 'YESTERDAY'?

ARE YOU LIVING YOUR PAST OVER AND OVER AGAIN?

WHAT IS KEEPING YOU IN THE PAST?

The Power of Three ~ Tomorrow

TODAY...

I TRAVEL TOWARD TOMORROW,

RELAXING IN THE MOMENT, BASKING IN THE VIEW.

Tomorrow

Figuring I shouldn't be caught up in my past, I jumped right from 'Yesterday' to thoughts, concerns, worries, dreams, and ambitions, anything that would take me to tomorrow.

What will tomorrow bring? How will I manifest what I want? What is my purpose for tomorrow?

Like a whirlwind, my mind darted from one thought to the next. Soon I learned that living in tomorrow means living in anxiety, living in imagination, which isn't real, as tomorrow isn't here. It doesn't exist as reality at the current moment.

Dreaming, planning, and setting goals for the future is reasonable. It's necessary even. However, always thinking of the future with worry and anxiety is not the right place to be. We have no control over the future as it's not here - yet. Being in a constant state of living for tomorrow isn't healthy either. Eventually, I discovered there was a better choice.

WHAT ARE YOUR THOUGHTS REGARDING 'TOMORROW'?

ARE YOU LIVING FOR TOMORROW WITHOUT ANY REGARD
OF WHAT TODAY WILL BRING?

WHAT IS KEEPING YOU IN THE FUTURE?

The Power of Three ~ Today

TODAY WASN'T YESTERDAY; I AM LETTING IT GO.

TODAY ISN'T TOMORROW; I AM NOT THERE.

TODAY IS HERE; I AM PRESENT NOW!

Today

I finally discovered 'Today.' Have you heard these terms before? The here and now; being present; in this moment; mindfully aware? All we have right now is today, this current moment in time.

In a healing session I once had with my Acupuncturist, we were discussing meditation and being present, and he said, "You realize, every person alive is only one breath away from death."

Isn't it magical that we never have to think consciously of our next breath unless we are fighting for it, or aware of it through breathing techniques or meditation?

When learning about today, I gained peace and joy. I have control over what I do, think, and feel within the next moments of today as the minutes unfold with me being aware of each one of them. It's like canoeing down a stream. When we paddle, coming upon each curve and current, we do so with control and command. It is at this moment we become aware of the journey of today.

WHAT ARE YOUR THOUGHTS REGARDING 'TODAY'?

HAVE YOU DISCOVERED TODAY?

ARE YOU HAPPY TODAY?

TODAY I AM...

IN THE MOMENT!

Journeying Back to Self

Over the years, life may lead you on a journey where you could feel like you're running out of control down a hill. Unable to catch your breath, afraid of falling and being badly hurt, you motor on without stopping.

Eventually, you're going to come to a halt. You'll look around, unable to understand the surrounding scenery and even worse who you are, where you've been or what you're expected to do next. Lost and alone, how do you find your way back to 'Self'?

Daily Practices

Through daily practices like becoming aware of your mindset, expressing gratitude, mindfulness, and meditation, and learning to let go of that which doesn't serve you anymore, you'll begin to discover a self that perhaps has been hidden for many years.

Do you take many things for granted? When was the last time you were grateful for everything in your life?

These practices take minimal time, some even less than five minutes a day, or as long as you need. Get to know yourself again. Become that friend to whom you once were.

TODAY I AM...
(WHAT ARE YOU WILLING TO DO TO JOURNEY BACK TO SELF?)

TODAY...
I CAN GO TWO DIRECTIONS;
I CAN STEP BACK INTO THE ABYSS
OR FORWARD INTO THE LIGHT.

The Spirit versus Ego

The ego is that part of the mind that is responsible for the sense of self. Ego gives us our self-importance. Many things we do and accomplish in life are ego driven. When doing the practices, to understand who you genuinely are, become wise to ideas, interpretations, or reality coming from your spirit versus ego. Spirit is your character and feelings, mood, determination, strength, and courage that stem from the energy of self, and that are not of your body.

TODAY I AM...

WHAT DO YOU WISH TO SAY TO EGO?

WHAT WOULD YOU LIKE SPIRIT TO KNOW?

28

Values and Change

One thing I learned as I did the practices daily, and this means letting things go, is that one's values change over time. Values are the standards and behaviors that you live your life by. These stem from how you were raised, the beliefs you grew up with, or the attitudes you picked up along your life's path.

I believe values change with life experiences, wisdom gained from those experiences, and with your current age. Don't be afraid to recognize your values from what they may have been several, or even a couple of years ago to what they are now. We change, and so do our values. It takes reflection to recognize the set of values we live with and how it defines us.

Take a few moments to consider the following statements.

TODAY I AM...

HOW HAVE YOUR VALUES CHANGED OVER THE YEARS?

WHAT CHANGES COULD YOU MAKE IN YOUR VALUE SYSTEM TO FIND YOUR WAY BACK TO SELF?

TODAY...

**I WELCOME SPIRIT WITH AN OPEN HEART;
LET HER COME DANCING OUT OF THE DARKNESS
AND INTO THE LIGHT.**

The Universe

Your belief system, and how you perceive yourself within this world guides who you are, and the choices you make. I use the term 'The Universe' here to describe that which is all-encompassing, everything that exists, and something which we can't see, but surrounds us and is known to us. You may choose to use the terms: God, Source Energy, Higher Power, Spirit, intuition, or another depending on your religion, culture, and belief system.

When I use The Universe, it's because I feel a higher power guides me in my life choices and how I succeed with them. My emotions depend on how I listen and follow my intuition or align with my soul's desires, passions, wants, needs, etc.

When working through the practices, you may wish to search for feelings, ideas, thoughts, and words which connect you to something much bigger than yourself such as _____.
(Write your specific term here, i.e., The Universe).

WHAT DO YOU CONNECT TO, WHICH IS MORE SIGNIFICANT THAN YOURSELF?

TODAY I AM...

OPENING MY EYES TO THE UNIVERSE,

TO SEE ALL THE BEAUTY SHE OFFERS.

AS I WALK ALONG THE PATH, I LOOK FOR A

SINGLE WHITE FEATHER TO KNOW

<u>I AM NOT ALONE.</u>

I SEEK THE SKY AND BILLOWING CLOUDS

FOR AN ANGEL WHO'S WATCHING OVER ME.

I LISTEN TO MY INNER VOICE WAITING

FOR IMAGINATION, INTUITION, AND PASSION

TO GUIDE ME ON MY JOURNEY –

THE NEXT STEP INTO THE UNKNOWN,

UNFALTERING AND SAFE.

TODAY I...

REALIZE THE HISTORY OF
MY PAST EXPERIENCES
MAKE ME WHO I AM;
RESPONSIVE TO CHANGE,
ALTHOUGH LEARNED
CHARACTERISTICS
BURIED DEEP WITHIN
MAY NEVER BE EXCAVATED.

Where I Am Today
(In This Present Moment)

Get All the 'Raw Stuff' Down

Ah, where to start. There's an old saying, "If you don't know where you've been, how will you know where you are going?". It's hard to change if you can't see what your thoughts and mindset are today. Sometimes you don't know a change is happening until you are in the middle of, or even far past the result. Today is what counts. Below is a simple exercise in letting it all out. There are no prompts, no suggestions. Write from your heart, no matter how positive or negative the result. What are you feeling today?

NOTE: Don't censor your thoughts, free write whatever comes to mind. Date this entry, so you'll know when you wrote it and what your thoughts were at this moment in time.

FIND YOURSELF A QUIET, UNINTERRUPTED SPOT AND SET A TIMER FOR 5 MINUTES. WRITE ANYTHING YOUR HEART WISHES TO SAY.

DATE:

Release

Doesn't it feel good to release, and acknowledge your thoughts? Release anything at this time which may not be serving your interest in creating a joyful and happy existence.

WRITE ANYTHING YOU WISH TO LET GO OF TODAY – THOSE THOUGHTS WHICH ONLY SERVE TO MAKE YOU UNHAPPY, SAD, DISGRUNTLED, WORRIED, AND ANGRY.

TODAY...

I SET THE FOUNDATION
FOR ALL MY TOMORROWS.

TODAY I AM...

HOW WILL YOU FINISH THIS STATEMENT?

ARE YOU READY TO FIND YOUR BLISS, JOY, AND HAPPINESS?

WHAT UPLIFTING THOUGHTS CAN YOU WRITE DOWN THAT WILL
PROPEL YOU TOWARD FUTURE POSITIVITY?

TODAY I AM...

Defining Your Joy

I knew when I began the journey back to myself, I needed to define 'joy' and what being joyful meant to me. I discovered that joy is different than happiness and being content. It is a state, not an emotion. It is a sense, a way of being, even if only captured for a moment. To me, while joy is close to happiness, it is more heart-centered.

In a world full of silence, Joy is music.

What Joy Means to Me

Joy arises in my life when I stop and smell the moment. Especially sensed most often when I'm taking a walk in nature. My most joyous moments have been sitting as one with Mother Nature. I let the wind caress my cheeks, smelling the earth, taking energy from within and making it sweep throughout my body, giving me life and hope for another tomorrow.

When I'm not alone, many simple acts create joy within me; sharing a smile, being kind, sensing a need to help and make another person or animal feel better. Joy is movement, a dance, a feel-good burst of energy floating throughout my body. Something magical happens to my heart and soul, where I sense with my whole being. I breathe energy in, sending it out mindfully and cherish the moment for what is, happy in the here and now, one with my body – JOY!

WHAT DOES JOY MEAN TO YOU?
WRITE IT HERE AS A REFERENCE AND RETURN TO IT OFTEN.

Defining Your Values Today

Your standards and behaviors are your values. Our parents teach us a set of values as we grow up. Once we're adults, though, we choose how we wish to behave and what standards we hold dear to our hearts. We entertain different value systems during certain stages of our lives.

You aren't who you were years ago, or even months ago, and you may not be the same tomorrow or months from now. Defining the values which you believe in today lets you know where you are at, and what is important to you 'today.'

WHAT ARE YOUR VALUES (STANDARDS AND BEHAVIORS) 'TODAY'?

Today I Am... Practices

Mindfulness Meditation

As discussed earlier, becoming mindful is being aware in the present moment. Many mindfulness meditations are on the Internet. These meditations involve breathing practices, becoming aware of the body and mind, relaxing the body and muscles, and letting go of mental images. To practice being mindful, use this meditation daily. You can start by staying in the meditation for a few minutes. After you're more comfortable, you could extend the time for ten minutes or longer.

1. Sit in a comfortable chair with feet on the floor and knees bent (if you're outside on grass, take your shoes and socks off so you can be grounded at the same time). Keep your upper body straight and in good posture. Your hands can rest on your thighs. You may close your eyes.

2. Ignore your thoughts and take note of your breathing. Slow down your breath, and on the inhale, notice that point where the air enters your nose and then slides down your esophagus and into your lungs, filling them. On the exhale, notice where the air moves out of your nose, and the lungs release. Become aware of each breath sliding in and out of your nose.

3. Thoughts will come, but as they do, imagine a creek flowing in front of you. As each idea comes, don't acknowledge or give it attention – send the thought to the stream and let it flow down the current and out of sight. Breathing with ease and awareness continue to allow each breath to come in and flow out of your nose.

4. If you begin stressing or ruminating over a thought, don't judge or berate yourself, send it off and let it move on down the creek and out of sight.

5. When you are ready to end your meditation, slowly bring your awareness back to your body, open your eyes and sit still for a few minutes, become conscious of your surroundings, and when ready, rise slowly and carry on with your activities.

It's not always convenient to sit and meditate. Depending on where you are, you can become mindful using the same practice (although you may choose to leave your eyes open).

The following are some examples:

1. Waiting in line, or for an appointment.

2. Riding public transportation: on buses, planes or trains.

3. When feeling anxious and out of control, emotions are raging one way or another.

4. When taking a walk, become aware of breath, of your surroundings, the ground, the sky, the wind on your face, how the air feels to your cheeks, noises that surround you.

5. In the shower or bath. Conscious breath, then awareness of water cascading over your body, the sensation of lathering soap, the temperature of the enclosure.

6. Doing household tasks. Relax, breathe, and become aware of what your hands, arms, and legs are doing.

The main goal is to let all thought float away. Don't get caught up in thinking.

BECOME BREATH AND RELAXATION.
BE AWARE OF ACTIVITY AND SURROUNDINGS
WITHOUT ANALYZING ANY FEELINGS THAT COME.

LET ANY WORRIES, FEARS, ANXIETY,
AND OTHER EMOTIONS GO.
BE MINDFUL OF THE MOMENT AS IT EXISTS.

Being 'In and Of Spirit'

Your spirit loves you!

It's time to find your way back to your spirit - that part of you which seeks harmony with your body and mind. It's your soul, psyche, character, and feelings all rolled into one. Consider your inner self and being filled with courage, determination, and willpower. You've heard of '...he/she has the spirit to go on.' Well, so do you!

There are many ways to honor your spirit. The practices listed here are all meant to engage in self-care, which is ongoing. When you show yourself some love, your soul has the power to heal.

Do these self-care practices. If you find it challenging to allow yourself some 'me' time, then set an appointment for yourself – a 'self-care' set time, and be sure to do it regularly!

1. Let go of things or activities which no longer serve you! Go over your life to-do list and chores. If something is no longer giving you joy, or is frustrating and bringing you down, let it go or find a workaround.

2. Learn to say, "NO." Doing so can be most liberating.

3. Ask yourself, "Am I doing this to please someone else without thought of how it will affect me?". If so… let it go, learn to say NO! (People pleasing is not allowed if you are putting yourself last - and NO you are not selfish!)

4. Take time to walk or hike in nature, or go to the park, beach, or countryside. While there, breathe and practice your mindfulness techniques.

5. Dance! Anywhere, anytime!

6. De-clutter. It's a great practice at the beginning of the year. Better yet, grab a box and put it in a corner year round. Whenever you come across anything you're not sure you need or want, hold the item and ask yourself, "Does this give me

TODAY...

I ALLOW SPIRIT TO TAKE FLIGHT, SETTING COURSE FOR A NEW DESTINATION OF LIGHT, LOVE, AND RESPECT FOR ME.

joy?". If it doesn't, put it in the box. When it's full, pass on the items, plan a garage sale, or give them to a second-hand store. Put another box in the corner and repeat. De-cluttering frees space and energy to allow new things to come to you.

7. Write a list to create rituals for 'me time.' Take a time out from regular activities — time to just 'be' for a few moments or several hours.

• You may want to meditate, journal, write, or read at a specific time each day or week.

• Perhaps, plan a bath night once a week, with candles, soft music, and low lighting. While in the bath, practice your mindfulness techniques.

• Plan spa days, picnics, long drives, vacations, and whatever other activities you can think of to gift yourself with some 'me time.'

• Make a list personal to your needs and schedule your 'me time' activities today!

GIVEN THIS LIST, TAKE TIME NOW TO PRIORITIZE ONE ITEM FROM ABOVE AND DO IT TODAY.

TODAY...

I LISTEN AND LOOK
WITH INNOCENCE
AND AWARENESS;
OF THOUGHT;
OF BODY;
OF SPIRIT;
OF VOICE;
OF SYMBOLISM –
TO HEAR AND SEE
THAT WHICH ENTERS
MY WORLD.

Being Innocent

One way of stepping into mindfulness is to look at things from a new perspective. To be innocent in the way we look at the world around us, similar to how a young child might view a butterfly or ladybug with fascination as if they've never seen one before. We take so much for granted, especially things which we pass by without thought or recognition. Do you travel the same journey to work every day, and never notice how different the sky looks?

When I was away at a week-long self-healing session, I walked down a back alley in a residential area each day to get to the workshop. It wasn't until the week was almost over that I finally lifted my head and looked around me. At that moment, I was walking past a back yard where the owners had built a little rock wall against their fence. They had painted the rocks with the message, "Have a nice day", and added some beautiful flower art and potted plants. When I noticed it, I felt such a sense of joy as I knew The Universe was speaking to me. With my head down the whole week, I was closed up, not looking at anything around me, so I missed the message. Imagine the things we miss by not being aware and being innocent to the sights, signals, and sounds that surround us.

THROUGH THE EYES OF INNOCENCE, LOOK OUTSIDE OF A WINDOW OR AT THE SPACE AROUND YOU. LIST ALL THE THINGS YOU SEE AND HEAR.

Have you noticed something new (even though it has been there all along)? Do you see beauty or find joy in what presents itself?

Setting Intentions

You are most likely setting intentions daily without even knowing it. Something where you determined you'd like a particular ending or result to happen. You set it in your mind and forget about it until much later when you realize it worked out exactly as planned. Setting an intention activates the conscious mind to receive that which is put forth and sets The Universe in motion to present that intention to you, showing how powerful thought and manifestation is.

Setting "the power of intention" is used by many healers, and in spiritual sessions to determine a specific outcome. It is a useful practice. You send an intention out into The Universe to attract a wish and then let it go. Today, we'll look at setting an intention that speaks to the mind, body, and spirit, rather than based on physical wants and needs. Be sure you're in a grateful state for all that you have currently, and where you are at the present moment. The results of intentions come when you are thankful and content, "putting it out there," rather than, "I want/need this; give it to me." You can set intentions for as long as you like, a day, week, month, or even for the year. If you are selecting a specific time, be sure to revisit it with feelings of love and connection.

THE FOLLOWING STEPS WILL AID YOU IN THE PRACTICE OF "SETTING AN INTENTION."

It's good practice to set and use intentions any time you wish.

1. FORM AN INTENTION (make it specific) during a quiet moment of reflection, after meditation, or upon waking, that serves your body, mind, or spirit in the present moment.

2. SET THE INTENTION by announcing it to The Universe. Use a ritual such as lighting a candle, placing your palm on your heart, having a bath, sitting in a meditative state, writing it in a journal, or simply breathing in the intention.

TODAY...

**I SET THE INTENTION OF LISTENING FOR
JUDGING THOUGHTS I PLACE UPON MYSELF
AND ABOUT OTHERS, RECOGNIZING THEM,
AND KNOWING THEY SERVE NO PURPOSE IN MY LIFE.**

3. LET IT GO and stop rehashing it over and over in your mind. By letting go of the intention, The Universe can do the magic it needs to bring it to light. If you've shared your purpose, don't let other people's negative thoughts or doubts detract from it. Allow your higher self to be receptive to the release of intention and that it will manifest exactly as it should.

4. RELEASE OUTCOMES, as your intention may or may not come to pass. It doesn't matter. Plan to have an unquestioning belief that what you put out into The Universe, you will receive.

5. TRUST IN THE UNIVERSE when using your 'letting go ritual' that everything will work out just as it should and that you know The Universe can handle all the details.

WHAT IS YOUR INTENTION TODAY?

Form an intention through reflection, set it by writing it here and then let it go ~ like the wind carrying a leaf into the air, there's no need to worry about where and when it will land.

TODAY...

I CELEBRATE ALL THAT I AM –
MY HEALTHY BODY,
MY CREATIVE MIND,
MY BOLD SPIRIT.
HELLO AWESOME ME!

Positive Affirmations

It took this author ages before I even felt remotely comfortable giving myself positive affirmations and compliments. The world is changing, but when I was growing up, compliments were few and far between unless they had to do with work, but never personal. It was far easier to degrade and berate oneself with bad inner dialogue than it was to be kind to oneself.

An affirmation is a statement or declaration. Positive affirmations impact the quality of our lives by the bright and confident messages they send to our soul, mind, and most of all, our spirit, and to The Universe in general. Being positive helps us to think better of ourselves and puts us in the right mindset and mood, motivating us to move forward. The affirmation, written in the present tense, states that we can be that which we declare. Rather than, "I will be successful," you'd write, "I am successful."

If you find it challenging to believe wholeheartedly in your positive affirmation, be sure to repeat it often in your mind. Better yet, write it down and come to understand its meaning, reviewing it and saying it often.

TODAY... WHAT IS YOUR POSITIVE AFFIRMATION REGARDING SELF?

Follow the Daily Practices in the, 365 Days of Today I Am...,
section, sending some positive affirmations out into The Universe.

TODAY...

WHAT A JOURNEY YOU'RE ON.
SPREAD YOUR SASSY LIGHT
AND LOVE FOR ALL THE WORLD
TO SEE IT BECAUSE IT'S BRILLIANT!

Notes to Self

Have you ever been fortunate enough to have a loved one leave a small handwritten message in your lunch, on your desk, or someplace else where you would find it? How did it make you feel when you read it? You can leave yourself notes of encouragement, reflection, and yes, even love.

You may want to write a positive note to yourself and place it where you can see it every day. A favorite quote you come across works well too. Jot it down for future reference. Be brave and tell yourself how you feel about you! Remember we are talking about positive messages.

When writing notes, you have the power to change your mindset to one of joy, freedom, and happiness only by what you tell yourself.

WRITE DOWN A THOUGHT THAT ISN'T SERVING YOU THE BEST RIGHT NOW.
(I.e., It's hard sharing information about myself when I first meet new people.)

HOW CAN YOU RE-FRAME IT INTO A POSITIVE THOUGHT?
(I.e., I have lots of exciting things to tell others about me.)

WRITE A NOTE TO YOURSELF STATING THE THOUGHT IN A POSITIVE LIGHT.
(I.e., I'm an attractive, loving person. Everyone deserves to learn who I am!)

TODAY...

WHEN I LOOKED IN THE MIRROR,
A GENTLE SOUL SMILED BACK AT ME.
I SAID, "HELLO, BEAUTIFUL!".

Mirror Talk

Mirror talk is similar to writing notes to yourself, but you will be looking directly into a mirror, into your eyes, and saying messages out loud to you. This powerful practice helps you come to love yourself or solidify love for yourself if it has been lacking. It goes back to self-talk and what we say to ourselves is what we come to believe.

Talking through our eyes to our subconscious establishes habits for positive thinking and believing in ourselves. We send healing thoughts and messages, and this brings about renewed self-confidence and self-esteem.

It is as easy as it sounds. When you're in front of the mirror, look directly into your eyes and speak positive affirmations. How often you wish to do this depends on your current thought patterns of self-love.

STAND IN FRONT OF A MIRROR AND LOOK DEEP INTO YOUR EYES. WHAT DO YOU SEE?

WHAT EMOTIONS DO YOU FEEL IN THE PRESENT MOMENT?

WHAT WILL YOU SAY TO YOU?

TODAY...

A BLANK CANVAS INVITES YOU TO CREATE YOUR VISION!

Creating a Vision Board

It is fun to create a vision board to help you manifest desires and wishes in your life. These are represented through images which you place any which way on a poster board or canvas. You can keep it in a visible place to look at, or meditate on it often. Work with your imagination to visualize that what you created on the board will manifest in real life. (As a side note, it is fun to do one without thought or concentration to see what visual messages come from your soul's intuition and The Universe.)

If you have access to a variety of magazines or artwork, begin by cutting out pictures, titles and sayings, even bits of paragraphs, and text. When you've got a bunch of clippings, gather together a large piece of poster board or canvas, scissors, and glue.

Search through the clippings and select what you wish to manifest (i.e., pictures of a new home, vacation, job type, love, friendship, etc.). If you are letting your subconscious pick for you, select anything which speaks to or resonates with you, but don't reflect too deeply or analyze the selection (you can do this once it's finished).

Place your pieces any way you wish on the board or canvas. When you feel the piece is finished and want to leave the layout as is, then use glue to secure the clippings in place. You can also use stickers, pens, felt pens, or crayons to add embellishments and artwork.

A great time to do a vision board is at the beginning of the New Year, or any time you feel the need and wish to create visual insights into your life.

GATHER A COLLECTION OF MAGAZINES AND ART CLIPPINGS.
SET A DATE TO MAKE A VISION BOARD.
INVITE A FEW FRIENDS OVER FOR A VISION BOARD PARTY.

It's fun to see how unique, and personal everyone's Vision Board will be.

26 Days of the Alphabet

This exercise is a fun little practice. For the next twenty-six days, using your own word choices, quickly jot down five or more positive words that begin with a letter of the alphabet from A to Z.

It is best to use your own word choice first as it comes to mind, but if you find it difficult and it's taking too long to come up with anything, use a dictionary, thesaurus or examples from the Word Selection list at the back of this journal. (Note 'x', and 'z' may be difficult. You could make up a unique word which reflects you).

Examples:

Date: 1/1/2019   Letter A
Today I am...
   appreciated, allowed, ample, anticipating, active

Date: 1/2/2019   Letter B
Today I am...
   bold, beautiful, bountiful, brazen, brilliant

DATE: ___ / ___ /20___ LETTER A
TODAY I AM...

DATE: ___ / ___ /20___ LETTER B
TODAY I AM...

DATE: ___ / ___ /20___ LETTER C
TODAY I AM...

DATE: ___ /___ /20___ LETTER D
TODAY I AM...

DATE: ___ /___ /20___ LETTER E
TODAY I AM...

DATE: ___ /___ /20___ LETTER F
TODAY I AM...

DATE: ___ /___ /20___ LETTER G
TODAY I AM...

DATE: ___ /___ /20___ LETTER H
TODAY I AM...

DATE: ___ /___ /20___ LETTER I
TODAY I AM...

DATE: ___ /___ /20___ LETTER J
TODAY I AM...

DATE: ___ / ___ /20___ LETTER K

TODAY I AM...

DATE: ___ / ___ /20___ LETTER L

TODAY I AM...

DATE: ___ / ___ /20___ LETTER M

TODAY I AM...

DATE: ___ / ___ /20___ LETTER N

TODAY I AM...

DATE: ___ / ___ /20___ LETTER O

TODAY I AM...

DATE: ___ / ___ /20___ LETTER P

TODAY I AM...

DATE: ___ / ___ /20___ LETTER Q

TODAY I AM...

DATE: ___ / ___ /20___ LETTER R

TODAY I AM...

DATE: ___ /___ /20___ LETTER S
TODAY I AM...

DATE: ___ /___ /20___ LETTER T
TODAY I AM...

DATE: ___ /___ /20___ LETTER U
TODAY I AM...

DATE: ___ /___ /20___ LETTER V
TODAY I AM...

DATE: ___ /___ /20___ LETTER W
TODAY I AM...

DATE: ___ /___ /20___ LETTER X
TODAY I AM...

DATE: ___ /___ /20___ LETTER Y
TODAY I AM...

DATE: ___ /___ /20___ LETTER Z
TODAY I AM...

365 Days of Daily Gratitude

When we don't acknowledge the things in life which we are grateful for, it is difficult to find happiness. Writing down anything no matter how large or small, detailed or simple, that we are thankful for will help us recognize not all is bad. We have some positive, awesome things in our lives, which we appreciate. It is best to be consistent (make a new morning routine), and take a few minutes to practice gratitude daily.

NOTE: Don't be afraid to dig deep and talk to your soul and The Universe. Doing this might take some practice, but it will happen eventually. The first example looks at life externally (when more profound words won't come). The second one takes a look at gratitude from your spirit and soul's perspective.

The following section, 365 Days of Daily Gratitude, allows for an entry every day. Get into the habit of doing this daily practice, and then over time, you'll find much more contentment, joy, peace, and happiness.

EXAMPLES:

This first example references everyday living and sometimes the things we most take for granted.

DATE: 1/1/2019
TODAY I AM... GRATEFUL FOR...

1. MY BED AND A GOOD NIGHT'S SLEEP.
2. A PHONE CALL FROM MY FRIEND.
3. FOOD, ABUNDANT, AND AVAILABLE.

AND... HAVING A GREAT FAMILY.

TODAY...

I'M GRATEFUL FOR THE GIFT OF BREATH,
LIVING THE BEST LIFE I KNOW HOW,
EXPANDING MY KNOWLEDGE AND
FINALLY BECOMING WHOLE AGAIN.

This second example reflects excavating those parts of our 'spirit' where we are truly grateful for what we've accomplished and how we're progressing in life.

DATE: 1/2/2019
TODAY I AM... GRATEFUL FOR...

1. RELEASING NEGATIVE ENERGY AND EMOTIONS AND CREATING A POSITIVE ENVIRONMENT TO SURROUND ME.

2. NEVER GIVING UP, ALWAYS MOVING FORWARD TO MAKE MY DREAMS SUCCEED.

3. LOVING MY PASSION AND THE DRIVE TO BE CREATIVE AND MAKE THINGS HAPPEN.

AND... SHARING MY EMPATHY TODAY WITH A KIND SMILE TO THOSE I MEET.

365 Days of Today I Am...

As discussed earlier, 'Today' is the most important day of your life. You are here, breathing, alive and in this moment. How are you feeling today?

The Today I Am…, practice is meant to be positive. Remember it is an affirmation that your subconscious is going to become aware of as you write it and as the day progresses.

Every morning, after writing your daily gratitude, also write a statement, or set of words, which will put you in a good mindset for continuing the rest your day.

You will find The 365 Days of Today I Am…, statements in the 365 Days of Daily Gratitude section. Allowing for an entry every day, be sure to write your Today I Am… affirmations. Get into the habit of doing this practice, and over time you'll find growth in self-confidence, peace, and contentment.

EXAMPLES:

DATE: 1/1/2019
TODAY I AM...
CONTENT, AT PEACE, IN A GREAT MINDSET WHICH BRINGS ME CALM, CENTERING, FOCUS, PASSION, AND PURPOSE.

DATE: 1/2/2019
TODAY I AM...
ENERGETIC, FOCUSED, PLEASANT, LOVED, CHERISHED, AND RESPECTED.

TODAY I AM...

BREATHING IN POSSIBILITIES –
LETTING GO OF ANY BLOCKAGES
THAT MAY BE HOLDING ME BACK.

TODAY I AM...

LIGHT, LOVE, RELAXED, BOUNTIFUL,
ENGAGED IN LIFE, ACCEPTING.

TODAY I AM...

MARVELING AT ALL LIFE'S OFFERINGS,
I LIVE IN A BEAUTIFUL WORLD.

DATE: ___ / ___ / 20___

TODAY I AM... GRATEFUL FOR...

1.

2.

3.

AND...

TODAY I AM...

DATE: ___ / ___ / 20___

TODAY I AM... GRATEFUL FOR...

1.

2.

3.

AND...

TODAY I AM...

DATE: ___ / ___ / 20___

TODAY I AM... GRATEFUL FOR...

1.

2.

3.

AND...

TODAY I AM...

DATE: ___ / ___ / 20 ___
TODAY I AM... GRATEFUL FOR...
1.
2.
3.
AND...

TODAY I AM...

DATE: ___ / ___ / 20 ___
TODAY I AM... GRATEFUL FOR...
1.
2.
3.
AND...

TODAY I AM...

DATE: ___ / ___ / 20 ___
TODAY I AM... GRATEFUL FOR...
1.
2.
3.
AND...

TODAY I AM...

DATE: ___ / ___ /20___
TODAY I AM... GRATEFUL FOR...
1.
2.
3.
AND...

TODAY I AM...

DATE: ___ / ___ /20___
TODAY I AM... GRATEFUL FOR...
1.
2.
3.
AND...

TODAY I AM...

DATE: ___ / ___ /20___
TODAY I AM... GRATEFUL FOR...
1.
2.
3.
AND...

TODAY I AM...

DATE: ___ /___ /20___
TODAY I AM... GRATEFUL FOR...
1.
2.
3.
AND...

TODAY I AM...

DATE: ___ /___ /20___
TODAY I AM... GRATEFUL FOR...
1.
2.
3.
AND...

TODAY I AM...

DATE: ___ /___ /20___
TODAY I AM... GRATEFUL FOR...
1.
2.
3.
AND...

TODAY I AM...

DATE: ___ /___ /20___
TODAY I AM... GRATEFUL FOR...
1.
2.
3.
AND...

TODAY I AM...

DATE: ___ /___ /20___
TODAY I AM... GRATEFUL FOR...
1.
2.
3.
AND...

TODAY I AM...

DATE: ___ /___ /20___
TODAY I AM... GRATEFUL FOR...
1.
2.
3.
AND...

TODAY I AM...

DATE: ___ / ___ / 20___
TODAY I AM... GRATEFUL FOR...
1.
2.
3.
AND...

TODAY I AM...

DATE: ___ / ___ / 20___
TODAY I AM... GRATEFUL FOR...
1.
2.
3.
AND...

TODAY I AM...

DATE: ___ / ___ / 20___
TODAY I AM... GRATEFUL FOR...
1.
2.
3.
AND...

TODAY I AM...

DATE: ___ / ___ /20___
TODAY I AM... GRATEFUL FOR...
1.
2.
3.
AND...

TODAY I AM...

DATE: ___ / ___ /20___
TODAY I AM... GRATEFUL FOR...
1.
2.
3.
AND...

TODAY I AM...

DATE: ___ / ___ /20___
TODAY I AM... GRATEFUL FOR...
1.
2.
3.
AND...

TODAY I AM...

DATE: ___ /___ /20___
TODAY I AM... GRATEFUL FOR...
1.
2.
3.
AND...

TODAY I AM...

DATE: ___ /___ /20___
TODAY I AM... GRATEFUL FOR...
1.
2.
3.
AND...

TODAY I AM...

DATE: ___ /___ /20___
TODAY I AM... GRATEFUL FOR...
1.
2.
3.
AND...

TODAY I AM...

DATE: ___ /___ /20___
TODAY I AM... GRATEFUL FOR...
1.
2.
3.
AND...

TODAY I AM...

DATE: ___ /___ /20___
TODAY I AM... GRATEFUL FOR...
1.
2.
3.
AND...

TODAY I AM...

DATE: ___ /___ /20___
TODAY I AM... GRATEFUL FOR...
1.
2.
3.
AND...

TODAY I AM...

DATE: ____ / ____ / 20 ____
TODAY I AM... GRATEFUL FOR...
1.
2.
3.
AND...

TODAY I AM...

DATE: ____ / ____ / 20 ____
TODAY I AM... GRATEFUL FOR...
1.
2.
3.
AND...

TODAY I AM...

DATE: ____ / ____ / 20 ____
TODAY I AM... GRATEFUL FOR...
1.
2.
3.
AND...

TODAY I AM...

DATE: ___ /___ /20___
TODAY I AM... GRATEFUL FOR...
1.
2.
3.
AND...

TODAY I AM...

DATE: ___ /___ /20___
TODAY I AM... GRATEFUL FOR...
1.
2.
3.
AND...

TODAY I AM...

DATE: ___ /___ /20___
TODAY I AM... GRATEFUL FOR...
1.
2.
3.
AND...

TODAY I AM...

DATE: ___ /___ /20___
TODAY I AM... GRATEFUL FOR...
1.
2.
3.
AND...

TODAY I AM...

DATE: ___ /___ /20___
TODAY I AM... GRATEFUL FOR...
1.
2.
3.
AND...

TODAY I AM...

DATE: ___ /___ /20___
TODAY I AM... GRATEFUL FOR...
1.
2.
3.
AND...

TODAY I AM...

DATE: ___ / ___ /20___
TODAY I AM... GRATEFUL FOR...
1.
2.
3.
AND...

TODAY I AM...

DATE: ___ / ___ /20___
TODAY I AM... GRATEFUL FOR...
1.
2.
3.
AND...

TODAY I AM...

DATE: ___ / ___ /20___
TODAY I AM... GRATEFUL FOR...
1.
2.
3.
AND...

TODAY I AM...

DATE: ___ / ___ /20___
TODAY I AM... GRATEFUL FOR...
1.
2.
3.
AND...

TODAY I AM...

DATE: ___ / ___ /20___
TODAY I AM... GRATEFUL FOR...
1.
2.
3.
AND...

TODAY I AM...

DATE: ___ / ___ /20___
TODAY I AM... GRATEFUL FOR...
1.
2.
3.
AND...

TODAY I AM...

DATE: ___/___/20___
TODAY I AM... GRATEFUL FOR...
1.
2.
3.
AND...

TODAY I AM...

DATE: ___/___/20___
TODAY I AM... GRATEFUL FOR...
1.
2.
3.
AND...

TODAY I AM...

DATE: ___/___/20___
TODAY I AM... GRATEFUL FOR...
1.
2.
3.
AND...

TODAY I AM...

DATE: ___ /___ /20___
TODAY I AM... GRATEFUL FOR...
1.
2.
3.
AND...

TODAY I AM...

DATE: ___ /___ /20___
TODAY I AM... GRATEFUL FOR...
1.
2.
3.
AND...

TODAY I AM...

DATE: ___ /___ /20___
TODAY I AM... GRATEFUL FOR...
1.
2.
3.
AND...

TODAY I AM...

DATE: ___ / ___ /20___
TODAY I AM... GRATEFUL FOR...
1.
2.
3.
AND...

TODAY I AM...

DATE: ___ / ___ /20___
TODAY I AM... GRATEFUL FOR...
1.
2.
3.
AND...

TODAY I AM...

DATE: ___ / ___ /20___
TODAY I AM... GRATEFUL FOR...
1.
2.
3.
AND...

TODAY I AM...

DATE: ___ /___ /20___
TODAY I AM... GRATEFUL FOR...
1.
2.
3.
AND...

TODAY I AM...

DATE: ___ /___ /20___
TODAY I AM... GRATEFUL FOR...
1.
2.
3.
AND...

TODAY I AM...

DATE: ___ /___ /20___
TODAY I AM... GRATEFUL FOR...
1.
2.
3.
AND...

TODAY I AM...

DATE: ___ /___ /20___
TODAY I AM... GRATEFUL FOR...
1.
2.
3.
AND...

TODAY I AM...

DATE: ___ /___ /20___
TODAY I AM... GRATEFUL FOR...
1.
2.
3.
AND...

TODAY I AM...

DATE: ___ /___ /20___
TODAY I AM... GRATEFUL FOR...
1.
2.
3.
AND...

TODAY I AM...

DATE: ___ /___ /20___
TODAY I AM... GRATEFUL FOR...
1.
2.
3.
AND...

TODAY I AM...

DATE: ___ /___ /20___
TODAY I AM... GRATEFUL FOR...
1.
2.
3.
AND...

TODAY I AM...

DATE: ___ /___ /20___
TODAY I AM... GRATEFUL FOR...
1.
2.
3.
AND...

TODAY I AM...

DATE: ___ /___ /20___
TODAY I AM... GRATEFUL FOR...
1.
2.
3.
AND...

TODAY I AM...

DATE: ___ /___ /20___
TODAY I AM... GRATEFUL FOR...
1.
2.
3.
AND...

TODAY I AM...

DATE: ___ /___ /20___
TODAY I AM... GRATEFUL FOR...
1.
2.
3.
AND...

TODAY I AM...

DATE: ___ /___ /20___
TODAY I AM... GRATEFUL FOR...
1.
2.
3.
AND...

TODAY I AM...

DATE: ___ /___ /20___
TODAY I AM... GRATEFUL FOR...
1.
2.
3.
AND...

TODAY I AM...

DATE: ___ /___ /20___
TODAY I AM... GRATEFUL FOR...
1.
2.
3.
AND...

TODAY I AM...

DATE: ___ / ___ /20___
TODAY I AM... GRATEFUL FOR...
1.
2.
3.
AND...

TODAY I AM...

DATE: ___ / ___ /20___
TODAY I AM... GRATEFUL FOR...
1.
2.
3.
AND...

TODAY I AM...

DATE: ___ / ___ /20___
TODAY I AM... GRATEFUL FOR...
1.
2.
3.
AND...

TODAY I AM...

DATE: ___/___/20___
TODAY I AM... GRATEFUL FOR...
1.
2.
3.
AND...

TODAY I AM...

DATE: ___/___/20___
TODAY I AM... GRATEFUL FOR...
1.
2.
3.
AND...

TODAY I AM...

DATE: ___/___/20___
TODAY I AM... GRATEFUL FOR...
1.
2.
3.
AND...

TODAY I AM...

DATE: ___ / ___ / 20___
TODAY I AM... GRATEFUL FOR...
1.
2.
3.
AND...

TODAY I AM...

DATE: ___ / ___ / 20___
TODAY I AM... GRATEFUL FOR...
1.
2.
3.
AND...

TODAY I AM...

DATE: ___ / ___ / 20___
TODAY I AM... GRATEFUL FOR...
1.
2.
3.
AND...

TODAY I AM...

DATE: ___ / ___ /20___
TODAY I AM... GRATEFUL FOR...
1.
2.
3.
AND...

TODAY I AM...

DATE: ___ / ___ /20___
TODAY I AM... GRATEFUL FOR...
1.
2.
3.
AND...

TODAY I AM...

DATE: ___ / ___ /20___
TODAY I AM... GRATEFUL FOR...
1.
2.
3.
AND...

TODAY I AM...

DATE: ___ /___ /20___
TODAY I AM... GRATEFUL FOR...
1.
2.
3.
AND...

TODAY I AM...

DATE: ___ /___ /20___
TODAY I AM... GRATEFUL FOR...
1.
2.
3.
AND...

TODAY I AM...

DATE: ___ /___ /20___
TODAY I AM... GRATEFUL FOR...
1.
2.
3.
AND...

TODAY I AM...

DATE: ___/___/20___
TODAY I AM... GRATEFUL FOR...
1.
2.
3.
AND...

TODAY I AM...

DATE: ___/___/20___
TODAY I AM... GRATEFUL FOR...
1.
2.
3.
AND...

TODAY I AM...

DATE: ___/___/20___
TODAY I AM... GRATEFUL FOR...
1.
2.
3.
AND...

TODAY I AM...

DATE: ___ / ___ /20___
TODAY I AM... GRATEFUL FOR...
1.
2.
3.
AND...

TODAY I AM...

DATE: ___ / ___ /20___
TODAY I AM... GRATEFUL FOR...
1.
2.
3.
AND...

TODAY I AM...

DATE: ___ / ___ /20___
TODAY I AM... GRATEFUL FOR...
1.
2.
3.
AND...

TODAY I AM...

DATE: ____ / ____ /20____
TODAY I AM... GRATEFUL FOR...
1.
2.
3.
AND...

TODAY I AM...

DATE: ____ / ____ /20____
TODAY I AM... GRATEFUL FOR...
1.
2.
3.
AND...

TODAY I AM...

DATE: ____ / ____ /20____
TODAY I AM... GRATEFUL FOR...
1.
2.
3.
AND...

TODAY I AM...

DATE: ____/____/20____
TODAY I AM... GRATEFUL FOR...
1.
2.
3.
AND...

TODAY I AM...

DATE: ____/____/20____
TODAY I AM... GRATEFUL FOR...
1.
2.
3.
AND...

TODAY I AM...

DATE: ____/____/20____
TODAY I AM... GRATEFUL FOR...
1.
2.
3.
AND...

TODAY I AM...

DATE: ___ / ___ / 20___
TODAY I AM... GRATEFUL FOR...
1.
2.
3.
AND...

TODAY I AM...

DATE: ___ / ___ / 20___
TODAY I AM... GRATEFUL FOR...
1.
2.
3.
AND...

TODAY I AM...

DATE: ___ / ___ / 20___
TODAY I AM... GRATEFUL FOR...
1.
2.
3.
AND...

TODAY I AM...

DATE: ___ /___ /20___
TODAY I AM... GRATEFUL FOR...
1.
2.
3.
AND...

TODAY I AM...

DATE: ___ /___ /20___
TODAY I AM... GRATEFUL FOR...
1.
2.
3.
AND...

TODAY I AM...

DATE: ___ /___ /20___
TODAY I AM... GRATEFUL FOR...
1.
2.
3.
AND...

TODAY I AM...

DATE: ___ /___ /20___
TODAY I AM... GRATEFUL FOR...
1.
2.
3.
AND...

TODAY I AM...

DATE: ___ /___ /20___
TODAY I AM... GRATEFUL FOR...
1.
2.
3.
AND...

TODAY I AM...

DATE: ___ /___ /20___
TODAY I AM... GRATEFUL FOR...
1.
2.
3.
AND...

TODAY I AM...

DATE: ___ /___ /20___
TODAY I AM... GRATEFUL FOR...
1.
2.
3.
AND...

TODAY I AM...

DATE: ___ /___ /20___
TODAY I AM... GRATEFUL FOR...
1.
2.
3.
AND...

TODAY I AM...

DATE: ___ /___ /20___
TODAY I AM... GRATEFUL FOR...
1.
2.
3.
AND...

TODAY I AM...

DATE: ___ /___ /20___
TODAY I AM... GRATEFUL FOR...
1.
2.
3.
AND...

TODAY I AM...

DATE: ___ /___ /20___
TODAY I AM... GRATEFUL FOR...
1.
2.
3.
AND...

TODAY I AM...

DATE: ___ /___ /20___
TODAY I AM... GRATEFUL FOR...
1.
2.
3.
AND...

TODAY I AM...

DATE: ___ / ___ / 20___
TODAY I AM... GRATEFUL FOR...
1.
2.
3.
AND...

TODAY I AM...

DATE: ___ / ___ / 20___
TODAY I AM... GRATEFUL FOR...
1.
2.
3.
AND...

TODAY I AM...

DATE: ___ / ___ / 20___
TODAY I AM... GRATEFUL FOR...
1.
2.
3.
AND...

TODAY I AM...

DATE: ____ / ____ / 20____

TODAY I AM... GRATEFUL FOR...

1.

2.

3.

AND...

TODAY I AM...

DATE: ____ / ____ / 20____

TODAY I AM... GRATEFUL FOR...

1.

2.

3.

AND...

TODAY I AM...

DATE: ____ / ____ / 20____

TODAY I AM... GRATEFUL FOR...

1.

2.

3.

AND...

TODAY I AM...

DATE: ____/____/20____
TODAY I AM... GRATEFUL FOR...
1.
2.
3.
AND...

TODAY I AM...

DATE: ____/____/20____
TODAY I AM... GRATEFUL FOR...
1.
2.
3.
AND...

TODAY I AM...

DATE: ____/____/20____
TODAY I AM... GRATEFUL FOR...
1.
2.
3.
AND...

TODAY I AM...

DATE: ____ /____ /20____
TODAY I AM... GRATEFUL FOR...
1.
2.
3.
AND...

TODAY I AM...

DATE: ____ /____ /20____
TODAY I AM... GRATEFUL FOR...
1.
2.
3.
AND...

TODAY I AM...

DATE: ____ /____ /20____
TODAY I AM... GRATEFUL FOR...
1.
2.
3.
AND...

TODAY I AM...

DATE: ___ /___ /20___
TODAY I AM... GRATEFUL FOR...
1.
2.
3.
AND...

TODAY I AM...

DATE: ___ /___ /20___
TODAY I AM... GRATEFUL FOR...
1.
2.
3.
AND...

TODAY I AM...

DATE: ___ /___ /20___
TODAY I AM... GRATEFUL FOR...
1.
2.
3.
AND...

TODAY I AM...

DATE: ___ /___ /20___
TODAY I AM... GRATEFUL FOR...
1.
2.
3.
AND...

TODAY I AM...

DATE: ___ /___ /20___
TODAY I AM... GRATEFUL FOR...
1.
2.
3.
AND...

TODAY I AM...

DATE: ___ /___ /20___
TODAY I AM... GRATEFUL FOR...
1.
2.
3.
AND...

TODAY I AM...

DATE: ____ / ____ / 20____
TODAY I AM... GRATEFUL FOR...
1.
2.
3.
AND...

TODAY I AM...

DATE: ____ / ____ / 20____
TODAY I AM... GRATEFUL FOR...
1.
2.
3.
AND...

TODAY I AM...

DATE: ____ / ____ / 20____
TODAY I AM... GRATEFUL FOR...
1.
2.
3.
AND...

TODAY I AM...

DATE: ___ /___ /20___
TODAY I AM... GRATEFUL FOR...
1.
2.
3.
AND...

TODAY I AM...

DATE: ___ /___ /20___
TODAY I AM... GRATEFUL FOR...
1.
2.
3.
AND...

TODAY I AM...

DATE: ___ /___ /20___
TODAY I AM... GRATEFUL FOR...
1.
2.
3.
AND...

TODAY I AM...

DATE: ___ / ___ /20___
TODAY I AM... GRATEFUL FOR...
1.
2.
3.
AND...

TODAY I AM...

DATE: ___ / ___ /20___
TODAY I AM... GRATEFUL FOR...
1.
2.
3.
AND...

TODAY I AM...

DATE: ___ / ___ /20___
TODAY I AM... GRATEFUL FOR...
1.
2.
3.
AND...

TODAY I AM...

DATE: ____ / ____ /20____

TODAY I AM... GRATEFUL FOR...

1.

2.

3.

AND...

TODAY I AM...

DATE: ____ / ____ /20____

TODAY I AM... GRATEFUL FOR...

1.

2.

3.

AND...

TODAY I AM...

DATE: ____ / ____ /20____

TODAY I AM... GRATEFUL FOR...

1.

2.

3.

AND...

TODAY I AM...

DATE: ____ / ____ /20____
TODAY I AM... GRATEFUL FOR...
1.
2.
3.
AND...

TODAY I AM...

DATE: ____ / ____ /20____
TODAY I AM... GRATEFUL FOR...
1.
2.
3.
AND...

TODAY I AM...

DATE: ____ / ____ /20____
TODAY I AM... GRATEFUL FOR...
1.
2.
3.
AND...

TODAY I AM...

DATE: ___/___/20___
TODAY I AM... GRATEFUL FOR...
1.
2.
3.
AND...

TODAY I AM...

DATE: ___/___/20___
TODAY I AM... GRATEFUL FOR...
1.
2.
3.
AND...

TODAY I AM...

DATE: ___/___/20___
TODAY I AM... GRATEFUL FOR...
1.
2.
3.
AND...

TODAY I AM...

DATE: ___ /___ /20___
TODAY I AM... GRATEFUL FOR...
1.
2.
3.
AND...

TODAY I AM...

DATE: ___ /___ /20___
TODAY I AM... GRATEFUL FOR...
1.
2.
3.
AND...

TODAY I AM...

DATE: ___ /___ /20___
TODAY I AM... GRATEFUL FOR...
1.
2.
3.
AND...

TODAY I AM...

DATE: ___ /___ /20___
TODAY I AM... GRATEFUL FOR...
1.
2.
3.
AND...

TODAY I AM...

DATE: ___ /___ /20___
TODAY I AM... GRATEFUL FOR...
1.
2.
3.
AND...

TODAY I AM...

DATE: ___ /___ /20___
TODAY I AM... GRATEFUL FOR...
1.
2.
3.
AND...

TODAY I AM...

DATE: ___ / ___ /20___
TODAY I AM... GRATEFUL FOR...
1.
2.
3.
AND...

TODAY I AM...

DATE: ___ / ___ /20___
TODAY I AM... GRATEFUL FOR...
1.
2.
3.
AND...

TODAY I AM...

DATE: ___ / ___ /20___
TODAY I AM... GRATEFUL FOR...
1.
2.
3.
AND...

TODAY I AM...

DATE: ___ /___ /20___
TODAY I AM... GRATEFUL FOR...
1.
2.
3.
AND...

TODAY I AM...

DATE: ___ /___ /20___
TODAY I AM... GRATEFUL FOR...
1.
2.
3.
AND...

TODAY I AM...

DATE: ___ /___ /20___
TODAY I AM... GRATEFUL FOR...
1.
2.
3.
AND...

TODAY I AM...

DATE: ___ /___ /20___
TODAY I AM... GRATEFUL FOR...
1.
2.
3.
AND...

TODAY I AM...

DATE: ___ /___ /20___
TODAY I AM... GRATEFUL FOR...
1.
2.
3.
AND...

TODAY I AM...

DATE: ___ /___ /20___
TODAY I AM... GRATEFUL FOR...
1.
2.
3.
AND...

TODAY I AM...

DATE: ___ /___ /20___
TODAY I AM... GRATEFUL FOR...
1.
2.
3.
AND...

TODAY I AM...

DATE: ___ /___ /20___
TODAY I AM... GRATEFUL FOR...
1.
2.
3.
AND...

TODAY I AM...

DATE: ___ /___ /20___
TODAY I AM... GRATEFUL FOR...
1.
2.
3.
AND...

TODAY I AM...

DATE: ___ /___ /20___
TODAY I AM... GRATEFUL FOR...
1.
2.
3.
AND...

TODAY I AM...

DATE: ___ /___ /20___
TODAY I AM... GRATEFUL FOR...
1.
2.
3.
AND...

TODAY I AM...

DATE: ___ /___ /20___
TODAY I AM... GRATEFUL FOR...
1.
2.
3.
AND...

TODAY I AM...

DATE: ____/____/20____

TODAY I AM... GRATEFUL FOR...

1.

2.

3.

AND...

TODAY I AM...

DATE: ____/____/20____

TODAY I AM... GRATEFUL FOR...

1.

2.

3.

AND...

TODAY I AM...

DATE: ____/____/20____

TODAY I AM... GRATEFUL FOR...

1.

2.

3.

AND...

TODAY I AM...

DATE: ___ /___ /20___
TODAY I AM... GRATEFUL FOR...
1.
2.
3.
AND...

TODAY I AM...

DATE: ___ /___ /20___
TODAY I AM... GRATEFUL FOR...
1.
2.
3.
AND...

TODAY I AM...

DATE: ___ /___ /20___
TODAY I AM... GRATEFUL FOR...
1.
2.
3.
AND...

TODAY I AM...

DATE: ___ /___ /20___
TODAY I AM... GRATEFUL FOR...
1.
2.
3.
AND...

TODAY I AM...

DATE: ___ /___ /20___
TODAY I AM... GRATEFUL FOR...
1.
2.
3.
AND...

TODAY I AM...

DATE: ___ /___ /20___
TODAY I AM... GRATEFUL FOR...
1.
2.
3.
AND...

TODAY I AM...

DATE: ___ /___ /20___
TODAY I AM... GRATEFUL FOR...
1.
2.
3.
AND...

TODAY I AM...

DATE: ___ /___ /20___
TODAY I AM... GRATEFUL FOR...
1.
2.
3.
AND...

TODAY I AM...

DATE: ___ /___ /20___
TODAY I AM... GRATEFUL FOR...
1.
2.
3.
AND...

TODAY I AM...

DATE: ___ / ___ /20___
TODAY I AM... GRATEFUL FOR...
1.
2.
3.
AND...

TODAY I AM...

DATE: ___ / ___ /20___
TODAY I AM... GRATEFUL FOR...
1.
2.
3.
AND...

TODAY I AM...

DATE: ___ / ___ /20___
TODAY I AM... GRATEFUL FOR...
1.
2.
3.
AND...

TODAY I AM...

DATE: ___ / ___ /20___
TODAY I AM... GRATEFUL FOR...
1.
2.
3.
AND...

TODAY I AM...

DATE: ___ / ___ /20___
TODAY I AM... GRATEFUL FOR...
1.
2.
3.
AND...

TODAY I AM...

DATE: ___ / ___ /20___
TODAY I AM... GRATEFUL FOR...
1.
2.
3.
AND...

TODAY I AM...

DATE: ___ /___ /20___
TODAY I AM... GRATEFUL FOR...
1.
2.
3.
AND...

TODAY I AM...

DATE: ___ /___ /20___
TODAY I AM... GRATEFUL FOR...
1.
2.
3.
AND...

TODAY I AM...

DATE: ___ /___ /20___
TODAY I AM... GRATEFUL FOR...
1.
2.
3.
AND...

TODAY I AM...

DATE: ___ /___ /20___
TODAY I AM... GRATEFUL FOR...
1.
2.
3.
AND...

TODAY I AM...

DATE: ___ /___ /20___
TODAY I AM... GRATEFUL FOR...
1.
2.
3.
AND...

TODAY I AM...

DATE: ___ /___ /20___
TODAY I AM... GRATEFUL FOR...
1.
2.
3.
AND...

TODAY I AM...

DATE: ___ / ___ /20___
TODAY I AM... GRATEFUL FOR...
1.
2.
3.
AND...

TODAY I AM...

DATE: ___ / ___ /20___
TODAY I AM... GRATEFUL FOR...
1.
2.
3.
AND...

TODAY I AM...

DATE: ___ / ___ /20___
TODAY I AM... GRATEFUL FOR...
1.
2.
3.
AND...

TODAY I AM...

DATE: ___ / ___ / 20___
TODAY I AM... GRATEFUL FOR...
1.
2.
3.
AND...

TODAY I AM...

DATE: ___ / ___ / 20___
TODAY I AM... GRATEFUL FOR...
1.
2.
3.
AND...

TODAY I AM...

DATE: ___ / ___ / 20___
TODAY I AM... GRATEFUL FOR...
1.
2.
3.
AND...

TODAY I AM...

DATE: ___ / ___ / 20___
TODAY I AM... GRATEFUL FOR...
1.
2.
3.
AND...

TODAY I AM...

DATE: ___ / ___ / 20___
TODAY I AM... GRATEFUL FOR...
1.
2.
3.
AND...

TODAY I AM...

DATE: ___ / ___ / 20___
TODAY I AM... GRATEFUL FOR...
1.
2.
3.
AND...

TODAY I AM...

DATE: ___/___/20___
TODAY I AM... GRATEFUL FOR...
1.
2.
3.
AND...

TODAY I AM...

DATE: ___/___/20___
TODAY I AM... GRATEFUL FOR...
1.
2.
3.
AND...

TODAY I AM...

DATE: ___/___/20___
TODAY I AM... GRATEFUL FOR...
1.
2.
3.
AND...

TODAY I AM...

DATE: ___ / ___ / 20___
TODAY I AM... GRATEFUL FOR...
1.
2.
3.
AND...

TODAY I AM...

DATE: ___ / ___ / 20___
TODAY I AM... GRATEFUL FOR...
1.
2.
3.
AND...

TODAY I AM...

DATE: ___ / ___ / 20___
TODAY I AM... GRATEFUL FOR...
1.
2.
3.
AND...

TODAY I AM...

DATE: ____ / ____ / 20____
TODAY I AM... GRATEFUL FOR...
1.
2.
3.
AND...

TODAY I AM...

DATE: ____ / ____ / 20____
TODAY I AM... GRATEFUL FOR...
1.
2.
3.
AND...

TODAY I AM...

DATE: ____ / ____ / 20____
TODAY I AM... GRATEFUL FOR...
1.
2.
3.
AND...

TODAY I AM...

DATE: ___ / ___ /20___
TODAY I AM... GRATEFUL FOR...
1.
2.
3.
AND...

TODAY I AM...

DATE: ___ / ___ /20___
TODAY I AM... GRATEFUL FOR...
1.
2.
3.
AND...

TODAY I AM...

DATE: ___ / ___ /20___
TODAY I AM... GRATEFUL FOR...
1.
2.
3.
AND...

TODAY I AM...

DATE: ___ /___ /20___
TODAY I AM... GRATEFUL FOR...
1.
2.
3.
AND...

TODAY I AM...

DATE: ___ /___ /20___
TODAY I AM... GRATEFUL FOR...
1.
2.
3.
AND...

TODAY I AM...

DATE: ___ /___ /20___
TODAY I AM... GRATEFUL FOR...
1.
2.
3.
AND...

TODAY I AM...

DATE: ___ /___ /20___
TODAY I AM... GRATEFUL FOR...
1.
2.
3.
AND...

TODAY I AM...

DATE: ___ /___ /20___
TODAY I AM... GRATEFUL FOR...
1.
2.
3.
AND...

TODAY I AM...

DATE: ___ /___ /20___
TODAY I AM... GRATEFUL FOR...
1.
2.
3.
AND...

TODAY I AM...

DATE: ___ /___ /20___
TODAY I AM... GRATEFUL FOR...
1.
2.
3.
AND...

TODAY I AM...

DATE: ___ /___ /20___
TODAY I AM... GRATEFUL FOR...
1.
2.
3.
AND...

TODAY I AM...

DATE: ___ /___ /20___
TODAY I AM... GRATEFUL FOR...
1.
2.
3.
AND...

TODAY I AM...

DATE: ____ / ____ /20____
TODAY I AM... GRATEFUL FOR...
1.
2.
3.
AND...

TODAY I AM...

DATE: ____ / ____ /20____
TODAY I AM... GRATEFUL FOR...
1.
2.
3.
AND...

TODAY I AM...

DATE: ____ / ____ /20____
TODAY I AM... GRATEFUL FOR...
1.
2.
3.
AND...

TODAY I AM...

DATE: ___ /___ /20___
TODAY I AM... GRATEFUL FOR...
1.
2.
3.
AND...

TODAY I AM...

DATE: ___ /___ /20___
TODAY I AM... GRATEFUL FOR...
1.
2.
3.
AND...

TODAY I AM...

DATE: ___ /___ /20___
TODAY I AM... GRATEFUL FOR...
1.
2.
3.
AND...

TODAY I AM...

DATE: ___ /___ /20___
TODAY I AM... GRATEFUL FOR...
1.
2.
3.
AND...

TODAY I AM...

DATE: ___ /___ /20___
TODAY I AM... GRATEFUL FOR...
1.
2.
3.
AND...

TODAY I AM...

DATE: ___ /___ /20___
TODAY I AM... GRATEFUL FOR...
1.
2.
3.
AND...

TODAY I AM...

DATE: ___ /___ /20___
TODAY I AM... GRATEFUL FOR...
1.
2.
3.
AND...

TODAY I AM...

DATE: ___ /___ /20___
TODAY I AM... GRATEFUL FOR...
1.
2.
3.
AND...

TODAY I AM...

DATE: ___ /___ /20___
TODAY I AM... GRATEFUL FOR...
1.
2.
3.
AND...

TODAY I AM...

DATE: ___ / ___ /20___
TODAY I AM... GRATEFUL FOR...
1.
2.
3.
AND...

TODAY I AM...

DATE: ___ / ___ /20___
TODAY I AM... GRATEFUL FOR...
1.
2.
3.
AND...

TODAY I AM...

DATE: ___ / ___ /20___
TODAY I AM... GRATEFUL FOR...
1.
2.
3.
AND...

TODAY I AM...

DATE: ___ / ___ / 20___
TODAY I AM... GRATEFUL FOR...
1.
2.
3.
AND...

TODAY I AM...

DATE: ___ / ___ / 20___
TODAY I AM... GRATEFUL FOR...
1.
2.
3.
AND...

TODAY I AM...

DATE: ___ / ___ / 20___
TODAY I AM... GRATEFUL FOR...
1.
2.
3.
AND...

TODAY I AM...

DATE: ___ /___ /20___
TODAY I AM... GRATEFUL FOR...
1.
2.
3.
AND...

TODAY I AM...

DATE: ___ /___ /20___
TODAY I AM... GRATEFUL FOR...
1.
2.
3.
AND...

TODAY I AM...

DATE: ___ /___ /20___
TODAY I AM... GRATEFUL FOR...
1.
2.
3.
AND...

TODAY I AM...

DATE: ___ /___ /20___
TODAY I AM... GRATEFUL FOR...
1.
2.
3.
AND...

TODAY I AM...

DATE: ___ /___ /20___
TODAY I AM... GRATEFUL FOR...
1.
2.
3.
AND...

TODAY I AM...

DATE: ___ /___ /20___
TODAY I AM... GRATEFUL FOR...
1.
2.
3.
AND...

TODAY I AM...

DATE: ___ /___ /20___
TODAY I AM... GRATEFUL FOR...
1.
2.
3.
AND...

TODAY I AM...

DATE: ___ /___ /20___
TODAY I AM... GRATEFUL FOR...
1.
2.
3.
AND...

TODAY I AM...

DATE: ___ /___ /20___
TODAY I AM... GRATEFUL FOR...
1.
2.
3.
AND...

TODAY I AM...

DATE: ___ / ___ / 20___
TODAY I AM... GRATEFUL FOR...
1.
2.
3.
AND...

TODAY I AM...

DATE: ___ / ___ / 20___
TODAY I AM... GRATEFUL FOR...
1.
2.
3.
AND...

TODAY I AM...

DATE: ___ / ___ / 20___
TODAY I AM... GRATEFUL FOR...
1.
2.
3.
AND...

TODAY I AM...

DATE: ___ /___ /20___
TODAY I AM... GRATEFUL FOR...
1.
2.
3.
AND...

TODAY I AM...

DATE: ___ /___ /20___
TODAY I AM... GRATEFUL FOR...
1.
2.
3.
AND...

TODAY I AM...

DATE: ___ /___ /20___
TODAY I AM... GRATEFUL FOR...
1.
2.
3.
AND...

TODAY I AM...

DATE: ____ /____ /20____
TODAY I AM... GRATEFUL FOR...
1.
2.
3.
AND...

TODAY I AM...

DATE: ____ /____ /20____
TODAY I AM... GRATEFUL FOR...
1.
2.
3.
AND...

TODAY I AM...

DATE: ____ /____ /20____
TODAY I AM... GRATEFUL FOR...
1.
2.
3.
AND...

TODAY I AM...

DATE: ____ /____ /20____
TODAY I AM... GRATEFUL FOR...
1.
2.
3.
AND...

TODAY I AM...

DATE: ____ /____ /20____
TODAY I AM... GRATEFUL FOR...
1.
2.
3.
AND...

TODAY I AM...

DATE: ____ /____ /20____
TODAY I AM... GRATEFUL FOR...
1.
2.
3.
AND...

TODAY I AM...

DATE: ___ /___ /20___
TODAY I AM... GRATEFUL FOR...
1.
2.
3.
AND...

TODAY I AM...

DATE: ___ /___ /20___
TODAY I AM... GRATEFUL FOR...
1.
2.
3.
AND...

TODAY I AM...

DATE: ___ /___ /20___
TODAY I AM... GRATEFUL FOR...
1.
2.
3.
AND...

TODAY I AM...

DATE: ___ / ___ /20___
TODAY I AM... GRATEFUL FOR...
1.
2.
3.
AND...

TODAY I AM...

DATE: ___ / ___ /20___
TODAY I AM... GRATEFUL FOR...
1.
2.
3.
AND...

TODAY I AM...

DATE: ___ / ___ /20___
TODAY I AM... GRATEFUL FOR...
1.
2.
3.
AND...

TODAY I AM...

DATE: ___ / ___ /20___
TODAY I AM... GRATEFUL FOR...
1.
2.
3.
AND...

TODAY I AM...

DATE: ___ / ___ /20___
TODAY I AM... GRATEFUL FOR...
1.
2.
3.
AND...

TODAY I AM...

DATE: ___ / ___ /20___
TODAY I AM... GRATEFUL FOR...
1.
2.
3.
AND...

TODAY I AM...

DATE: ___ /___ /20___
TODAY I AM... GRATEFUL FOR...
1.
2.
3.
AND...

TODAY I AM...

DATE: ___ /___ /20___
TODAY I AM... GRATEFUL FOR...
1.
2.
3.
AND...

TODAY I AM...

DATE: ___ /___ /20___
TODAY I AM... GRATEFUL FOR...
1.
2.
3.
AND...

TODAY I AM...

DATE: ___ /___ /20___
TODAY I AM... GRATEFUL FOR...
1.
2.
3.
AND...

TODAY I AM...

DATE: ___ /___ /20___
TODAY I AM... GRATEFUL FOR...
1.
2.
3.
AND...

TODAY I AM...

DATE: ___ /___ /20___
TODAY I AM... GRATEFUL FOR...
1.
2.
3.
AND...

TODAY I AM...

DATE: ___ / ___ /20___
TODAY I AM... GRATEFUL FOR...
1.
2.
3.
AND...

TODAY I AM...

DATE: ___ / ___ /20___
TODAY I AM... GRATEFUL FOR...
1.
2.
3.
AND...

TODAY I AM...

DATE: ___ / ___ /20___
TODAY I AM... GRATEFUL FOR...
1.
2.
3.
AND...

TODAY I AM...

DATE: ___ /___ /20___
TODAY I AM... GRATEFUL FOR...
1.
2.
3.
AND...

TODAY I AM...

DATE: ___ /___ /20___
TODAY I AM... GRATEFUL FOR...
1.
2.
3.
AND...

TODAY I AM...

DATE: ___ /___ /20___
TODAY I AM... GRATEFUL FOR...
1.
2.
3.
AND...

TODAY I AM...

DATE: ___ /___ /20___
TODAY I AM... GRATEFUL FOR...
1.
2.
3.
AND...

TODAY I AM...

DATE: ___ /___ /20___
TODAY I AM... GRATEFUL FOR...
1.
2.
3.
AND...

TODAY I AM...

DATE: ___ /___ /20___
TODAY I AM... GRATEFUL FOR...
1.
2.
3.
AND...

TODAY I AM...

DATE: ___ /___ /20___
TODAY I AM... GRATEFUL FOR...
1.
2.
3.
AND...

TODAY I AM...

DATE: ___ /___ /20___
TODAY I AM... GRATEFUL FOR...
1.
2.
3.
AND...

TODAY I AM...

DATE: ___ /___ /20___
TODAY I AM... GRATEFUL FOR...
1.
2.
3.
AND...

TODAY I AM...

DATE: ___ /___ /20___
TODAY I AM... GRATEFUL FOR...
1.
2.
3.
AND...

TODAY I AM...

DATE: ___ /___ /20___
TODAY I AM... GRATEFUL FOR...
1.
2.
3.
AND...

TODAY I AM...

DATE: ___ /___ /20___
TODAY I AM... GRATEFUL FOR...
1.
2.
3.
AND...

TODAY I AM...

DATE: ___ / ___ /20___
TODAY I AM... GRATEFUL FOR...
1.
2.
3.
AND...

TODAY I AM...

DATE: ___ / ___ /20___
TODAY I AM... GRATEFUL FOR...
1.
2.
3.
AND...

TODAY I AM...

DATE: ___ / ___ /20___
TODAY I AM... GRATEFUL FOR...
1.
2.
3.
AND...

TODAY I AM...

DATE: ____ / ____ /20____
TODAY I AM... GRATEFUL FOR...
1.
2.
3.
AND...

TODAY I AM...

DATE: ____ / ____ /20____
TODAY I AM... GRATEFUL FOR...
1.
2.
3.
AND...

TODAY I AM...

DATE: ____ / ____ /20____
TODAY I AM... GRATEFUL FOR...
1.
2.
3.
AND...

TODAY I AM...

DATE: ___ / ___ /20___
TODAY I AM... GRATEFUL FOR...
1.
2.
3.
AND...

TODAY I AM...

DATE: ___ / ___ /20___
TODAY I AM... GRATEFUL FOR...
1.
2.
3.
AND...

TODAY I AM...

DATE: ___ / ___ /20___
TODAY I AM... GRATEFUL FOR...
1.
2.
3.
AND...

TODAY I AM...

DATE: ___ / ___ / 20___
TODAY I AM... GRATEFUL FOR...
1.
2.
3.
AND...

TODAY I AM...

DATE: ___ / ___ / 20___
TODAY I AM... GRATEFUL FOR...
1.
2.
3.
AND...

TODAY I AM...

DATE: ___ / ___ / 20___
TODAY I AM... GRATEFUL FOR...
1.
2.
3.
AND...

TODAY I AM...

DATE: ___ / ___ /20___
TODAY I AM... GRATEFUL FOR...
1.
2.
3.
AND...

TODAY I AM...

DATE: ___ / ___ /20___
TODAY I AM... GRATEFUL FOR...
1.
2.
3.
AND...

TODAY I AM...

DATE: ___ / ___ /20___
TODAY I AM... GRATEFUL FOR...
1.
2.
3.
AND...

TODAY I AM...

DATE: ___ / ___ /20___
TODAY I AM... GRATEFUL FOR...
1.
2.
3.
AND...

TODAY I AM...

DATE: ___ / ___ /20___
TODAY I AM... GRATEFUL FOR...
1.
2.
3.
AND...

TODAY I AM...

DATE: ___ / ___ /20___
TODAY I AM... GRATEFUL FOR...
1.
2.
3.
AND...

TODAY I AM...

DATE: ____ /____ /20____
TODAY I AM... GRATEFUL FOR...
1.
2.
3.
AND...

TODAY I AM...

DATE: ____ /____ /20____
TODAY I AM... GRATEFUL FOR...
1.
2.
3.
AND...

TODAY I AM...

DATE: ____ /____ /20____
TODAY I AM... GRATEFUL FOR...
1.
2.
3.
AND...

TODAY I AM...

DATE: ___ / ___ / 20___
TODAY I AM... GRATEFUL FOR...
1.
2.
3.
AND...

TODAY I AM...

DATE: ___ / ___ / 20___
TODAY I AM... GRATEFUL FOR...
1.
2.
3.
AND...

TODAY I AM...

DATE: ___ / ___ / 20___
TODAY I AM... GRATEFUL FOR...
1.
2.
3.
AND...

TODAY I AM...

DATE: ____ / ____ /20____
TODAY I AM... GRATEFUL FOR...
1.
2.
3.
AND...

TODAY I AM...

DATE: ____ / ____ /20____
TODAY I AM... GRATEFUL FOR...
1.
2.
3.
AND...

TODAY I AM...

DATE: ____ / ____ /20____
TODAY I AM... GRATEFUL FOR...
1.
2.
3.
AND...

TODAY I AM...

DATE: ___ / ___ / 20 ___

TODAY I AM... GRATEFUL FOR...

1.

2.

3.

AND...

TODAY I AM...

DATE: ___ / ___ / 20 ___

TODAY I AM... GRATEFUL FOR...

1.

2.

3.

AND...

TODAY I AM...

DATE: ___ / ___ / 20 ___

TODAY I AM... GRATEFUL FOR...

1.

2.

3.

AND...

TODAY I AM...

DATE: ___/___/20___
TODAY I AM... GRATEFUL FOR...
1.
2.
3.
AND...

TODAY I AM...

DATE: ___/___/20___
TODAY I AM... GRATEFUL FOR...
1.
2.
3.
AND...

TODAY I AM...

DATE: ___/___/20___
TODAY I AM... GRATEFUL FOR...
1.
2.
3.
AND...

TODAY I AM...

DATE: ___ /___ /20___
TODAY I AM... GRATEFUL FOR...
1.
2.
3.
AND...

TODAY I AM...

DATE: ___ /___ /20___
TODAY I AM... GRATEFUL FOR...
1.
2.
3.
AND...

TODAY I AM...

DATE: ___ /___ /20___
TODAY I AM... GRATEFUL FOR...
1.
2.
3.
AND...

TODAY I AM...

DATE: ___ / ___ /20___
TODAY I AM... GRATEFUL FOR...
1.
2.
3.
AND...

TODAY I AM...

DATE: ___ / ___ /20___
TODAY I AM... GRATEFUL FOR...
1.
2.
3.
AND...

TODAY I AM...

DATE: ___ / ___ /20___
TODAY I AM... GRATEFUL FOR...
1.
2.
3.
AND...

TODAY I AM...

DATE: ___ /___ /20___
TODAY I AM... GRATEFUL FOR...
1.
2.
3.
AND...

TODAY I AM...

DATE: ___ /___ /20___
TODAY I AM... GRATEFUL FOR...
1.
2.
3.
AND...

TODAY I AM...

DATE: ___ /___ /20___
TODAY I AM... GRATEFUL FOR...
1.
2.
3.
AND...

TODAY I AM...

DATE: ___ /___ /20___
TODAY I AM... GRATEFUL FOR...
1.
2.
3.
AND...

TODAY I AM...

DATE: ___ /___ /20___
TODAY I AM... GRATEFUL FOR...
1.
2.
3.
AND...

TODAY I AM...

DATE: ___ /___ /20___
TODAY I AM... GRATEFUL FOR...
1.
2.
3.
AND...

TODAY I AM...

DATE: ___ /___ /20___
TODAY I AM... GRATEFUL FOR...
1.
2.
3.
AND...

TODAY I AM...

DATE: ___ /___ /20___
TODAY I AM... GRATEFUL FOR...
1.
2.
3.
AND...

TODAY I AM...

DATE: ___ /___ /20___
TODAY I AM... GRATEFUL FOR...
1.
2.
3.
AND...

TODAY I AM...

DATE: ___ /___ /20___
TODAY I AM... GRATEFUL FOR...
1.
2.
3.
AND...

TODAY I AM...

DATE: ___ /___ /20___
TODAY I AM... GRATEFUL FOR...
1.
2.
3.
AND...

TODAY I AM...

DATE: ___ /___ /20___
TODAY I AM... GRATEFUL FOR...
1.
2.
3.
AND...

TODAY I AM...

DATE: ___ /___ /20___
TODAY I AM... GRATEFUL FOR...
1.
2.
3.
AND...

TODAY I AM...

DATE: ___ /___ /20___
TODAY I AM... GRATEFUL FOR...
1.
2.
3.
AND...

TODAY I AM...

DATE: ___ /___ /20___
TODAY I AM... GRATEFUL FOR...
1.
2.
3.
AND...

TODAY I AM...

DATE: ___ /___ /20___
TODAY I AM... GRATEFUL FOR...
1.
2.
3.
AND...

TODAY I AM...

DATE: ___ /___ /20___
TODAY I AM... GRATEFUL FOR...
1.
2.
3.
AND...

TODAY I AM...

DATE: ___ /___ /20___
TODAY I AM... GRATEFUL FOR...
1.
2.
3.
AND...

TODAY I AM...

DATE: ____ /____ /20____
TODAY I AM... GRATEFUL FOR...
1.
2.
3.
AND...

TODAY I AM...

DATE: ____ /____ /20____
TODAY I AM... GRATEFUL FOR...
1.
2.
3.
AND...

TODAY I AM...

DATE: ____ /____ /20____
TODAY I AM... GRATEFUL FOR...
1.
2.
3.
AND...

TODAY I AM...

DATE: ___ /___ /20___
TODAY I AM... GRATEFUL FOR...
1.
2.
3.
AND...

TODAY I AM...

DATE: ___ /___ /20___
TODAY I AM... GRATEFUL FOR...
1.
2.
3.
AND...

TODAY I AM...

DATE: ___ /___ /20___
TODAY I AM... GRATEFUL FOR...
1.
2.
3.
AND...

TODAY I AM...

DATE: ____/____/20____
TODAY I AM... GRATEFUL FOR...
1.
2.
3.
AND...

TODAY I AM...

DATE: ____/____/20____
TODAY I AM... GRATEFUL FOR...
1.
2.
3.
AND...

TODAY I AM...

DATE: ____/____/20____
TODAY I AM... GRATEFUL FOR...
1.
2.
3.
AND...

TODAY I AM...

DATE: ___ /___ /20___
TODAY I AM... GRATEFUL FOR...
1.
2.
3.
AND...

TODAY I AM...

DATE: ___ /___ /20___
TODAY I AM... GRATEFUL FOR...
1.
2.
3.
AND...

TODAY I AM...

DATE: ___ /___ /20___
TODAY I AM... GRATEFUL FOR...
1.
2.
3.
AND...

TODAY I AM...

DATE: ___ /___ /20___
TODAY I AM... GRATEFUL FOR...
1.
2.
3.
AND...

TODAY I AM...

DATE: ___ /___ /20___
TODAY I AM... GRATEFUL FOR...
1.
2.
3.
AND...

TODAY I AM...

DATE: ___ /___ /20___
TODAY I AM... GRATEFUL FOR...
1.
2.
3.
AND...

TODAY I AM...

DATE: ____/____/20____
TODAY I AM... GRATEFUL FOR...
1.
2.
3.
AND...

TODAY I AM...

DATE: ____/____/20____
TODAY I AM... GRATEFUL FOR...
1.
2.
3.
AND...

TODAY I AM...

DATE: ____/____/20____
TODAY I AM... GRATEFUL FOR...
1.
2.
3.
AND...

TODAY I AM...

DATE: ___ /___ /20___
TODAY I AM... GRATEFUL FOR...
1.
2.
3.
AND...

TODAY I AM...

DATE: ___ /___ /20___
TODAY I AM... GRATEFUL FOR...
1.
2.
3.
AND...

TODAY I AM...

CONGRATULATIONS!
YOU'VE NOW COMPLETED A YEAR, THAT'S 365 DAYS OF
TODAY I AM...
DAILY GRATITUDE AND POSITIVE AFFIRMATIONS!

HOW HAS YOUR LIFE CHANGED?

Growth and Reflection

Where are you now as you've journeyed through and completed the practices in this journal? Have you gained insights about yourself you didn't know existed? Have you changed?

Perhaps several months and hopefully a year has gone by, and it's time to do a check-in. Remember, in the beginning, you were asked to "Get all the 'raw stuff' down..." and you dated the entry. It's time to do that again. This time write with the mindset of how far you've grown since starting the practices listed in this journal.

As stated throughout the sections, 'Today is what counts.' Write from your heart, what you are feeling today after completing the practices and see what you put down compared to what you once wrote a while ago.

NOTE: Don't censor your thoughts, free write your growth and reflections of whatever comes to mind. Date this entry, so you'll know when you wrote it and what your thoughts were at this moment in time.

FIND YOURSELF A QUIET, UNINTERRUPTED SPOT
AND SET A CLOCK TIMER FOR 5 MINUTES.
WRITE ANYTHING YOU ARE FEELING AND THINKING AT THIS MOMENT.

DATE:

HOW HAVE YOU GROWN TOWARD JOY AND HAPPINESS?

Word Selections
(When you can't find the word you want.)

The following words, listed alphabetically will help you in your **TODAY I AM...** practices. You'll note that all words are positive, uplifting, and have a strong character base.

When doing your practices, if you aren't able to come up with an accurate description of what you are feeling in the moment, take a look at this list. If you feel like adding words for future reference, then do so!

A...

able
accepted
achieving
active
adaptive
adjusted
adored
adventurous
agile
aligned
alive
allowed
amazed
amazing
ambitious
amused
appealing
appreciated
artistic
attentive
authentic
awake
awesome

B...

balanced
beaming
beautiful
becoming
believable
believing
beloved
bemused
better
blessed
blissful
blossoming
bold
bountiful
brave
brazen
breathing
bright
brilliant
broad-minded

C...

calm
capable
carefree
caring
centered
charismatic
charming
cheerful
cherished
childlike
chosen
clear
colorful
complete
confident
content
courageous
creative
credible
curious

D...

dancing
dapper
daring
dashing
dazzled
dear
dedicated
deep
defined
delectable
delightful
demanding
deserving
desired
determined
direct
divine
doing
dreaming
dynamic

WORDS/PHRASES FOR FUTURE REFERENCE

E...

eager
educated
empathetic
empowered
enabled
endless
energetic
energy
engaged
enjoyable
enlightened
enough
enthusiastic
excited
expressive

F...

fair
faithful
familiar
famous
far-seeing
fearless
feeling
filled
focused
forgiving
forthcoming
fortunate
found
free
friendly
fulfilled
fun
functioning
funny

WORDS/PHRASES FOR FUTURE REFERENCE

G...

gaining
generous
genuine
gifted
giving
glamorous
glorious
glowing
good
gracious
grand
grateful
great
grounded
growing
growth

H...

handsome
handy
happy
harmonious
headstrong
healed
healing
healthy
hearty
helpful
heroic
hilarious
holistic
honest
honorable
hopeful
humble
humorous

WORDS/PHRASES FOR FUTURE REFERENCE

I...

idyllic
ignited
imaginative
imagining
important
improved
incredible
independent
indispensable
industrious
innovative
inspired
intellectual
intelligent
intense
interested
interesting
invested
involved

J...

jaunty
jazzy
jolly
journeying
jovial
joy
joyful
jubilant

WORDS/PHRASES FOR FUTURE REFERENCE

K...

keen
kind
kinetic
king
knowing
knowledgeable

L...

laughing
leading
learning
letting
light
likable
limitless
listening
lively
living
love
lovable
loved
lovely
loving
loyal
lush

WORDS/PHRASES FOR FUTURE REFERENCE

M...

magical
magnificent
majestic
marvelous
mighty
more
motivated
multi-faceted
mushy
musing
mysterious
mystical

N...

naked
natural
necessary
new
nice
noble
normal
nourished
nourishing
nurtured

WORDS/PHRASES FOR FUTURE REFERENCE

O...

offering
okay
open
open-hearted
open-minded
opportunistic
optimistic
organized
original
overjoyed

P...

passionate
patient
peaceful
perfect
perfection
playful
pleased
plenty
positive
powerful
present
pretty
profound
progressing
proud
pure

WORDS/PHRASES FOR FUTURE REFERENCE

Q...

quaint
qualified
quick
quiet
quirky

R...

rare
ready
realizing
receiving
recognized
redeemed
redefining
refreshed
remarkable
replenished
resilient
resourceful
respected
rested
rich
rising
rooted

WORDS/PHRASES FOR FUTURE REFERENCE

S...

sacred
safe
satisfied
secure
seeing
seeking
sensing
sensual
serene
shining
significant
soulful
special
spirited
spiritual
striving
strong
successful
supported
sympathetic

T...

tangible
tender
testing
thankful
thoughtful
thriving
timely
together
total
tough
tranquil
trendy
truth
truthful

WORDS/PHRASES FOR FUTURE REFERENCE

U...

ultimate
unabashed
unafraid
unbeatable
unbreakable
uncontrolled
understanding
understood
unique
universal
unlimited
unselfish
unstoppable
unusual
unwavering
up
upbeat
uplifted
useful

V...

valuable
varying
venerable
versed
very…
vibrant
vigorous
visible
visiting
vital
vivacious
vivid
vocal
voluptuous
voracious

WORDS/PHRASES FOR FUTURE REFERENCE

W...

wacky
wandering
warm-hearted
warrior-like
wealthy
welcoming
well
whole
whole-hearted
wholesome
willing
winning
wise
wishful
wishing
witty
wonderful
wondering
worthy

X...

x-amining
x-amplifying
x-cellent
x-treme

Y...

yearning
young
youthful

Z...

zany
zealous
Zen-like
zesty
zippy

WORDS/PHRASES FOR FUTURE REFERENCE

TODAY I...

REALIZE YESTERDAY IS GONE;
TOMORROW HAS NOT YET ARRIVED;
AND AT THIS MOMENT, I SIMPLY

AM.

Notes

NOTES

NOTES

TODAY I AM...

EXPLORING THE WORLD,
LEARNING TO APPRECIATE
LOVE AND LAUGHTER,
AND CELEBRATING LIFE!

ABOUT PATRICIA L. ATCHISON

Writing has been my voice over several decades. I found a fascination with the subject of English throughout high school. After, I went on to take Journalism and expanded into Graphic Arts. Working with computers tweaked my interest, and I became a Systems Analyst for a major oil company. While there, I loved writing documentation for projects.

An opportunity arrived to take a course on Writing for Children and Young Adults. I said goodbye to the corporate world, although I didn't immediately jump into the young adult and children's writing genres. At the time, a hobby of mine was creating and making artist teddy bear collectibles. Drawing on my writing passion, I decided to challenge my skills through magazine publishing and created the Canadian Teddy Bear News magazine for artists and collectors.

Next, I delved into children's fiction, writing short stories. I self-published two children's books: Little Blue Penguin; and McKenzie's Frosty Surprise. Also, a guide: How to Write for Children, An Easy Three-Step Guide to Writing Children's Books.

After several years' hiatus, I'm currently writing again in various genres. These include delving into fantastical, post-apocalyptic, and dystopian ideas and writing non-fiction. In recent years, I've written a couple of young adult manuscripts, which are awaiting editing, and I've had many essay articles published.

My best writing comes from my heart, and that is why I decided to publish this journal. My life has had many highs and some deep lows, which is the same for everyone who walks this Earth. I wanted to share the tools I've learned, with the intention that if even one person gains something from this journal, the compilation will be worth it. My writing is quite like that. If one person reads and enjoys, or receives, from what I've written, I feel I've accomplished my goal of being an author and sharing my voice.

TODAY I AM...

AN EMPOWERING JOURNAL BACK TO SELF

If this journal has helped you find your way toward
self-confidence, improved self-esteem,
happiness, gratitude and joy-filled life experiences,
I'd love to hear your comments!

Please Visit:
www.patriciaatchisonauthor.com

Special sign-up for news, updates, and free downloads:

Please Visit:
land.patriciaatchison.ca/newsupdates

I'D LOVE TO CONNECT WITH YOU!

66510829R00116

Made in the USA
Middletown, DE
12 September 2019